A Literary Diva's Guide to Hosting a Fab Book Club Meeting

A Reference Guide for Planning an Interactive Book Discussion

Joy Farrington

A Literary Diva

Joy Farrington is CEO of Nubian Literary Network and president of Nubian Sistas Book Club. She is the moderator of Review Divas, Book Review Team and has been nominated for several literary awards. She lives in Miami, Florida. For information regarding book signings, workshops, and other speaking engagements, please contact us at nubianlit@gmail.com.

A Literary Diva's Guide to Hosting a Fab Book Club Meeting
Copyright © 2009 by Joy Farrington

ISBN: 978-0-557-26027-0

Printed in the USA by Lulu.com

Nubian Lit Publishing
18520 NW 67th Ave
Suite 241
Miami, Fl 33015
nubianlit@gmail.com

This book is dedicated to my son, Daelon,
growing stronger and smarter every day.
Mommy loves you.

and

To my brother, Ferron,
resting in peace in the City of Angels.
I miss you.

Acknowledgments

To my son, Daelon for being my motivation, my heart, my everything.

To my family: my sister, Michaelle, my cousins, Crystal, Keisha, Monique, Nicky, Sean, Sainabou, broh-in law, Ralph, my aunts, uncles, grandma and my parents, Jo and Mikey, thank you for always being in my corner and supporting all my crazy idea- well most of them anyways.

To my BFFs, Nicky D., and Mac, "you're not always there when I call, but you're always on time." I LOVE YOU MAN, lol.

To my editor, Pittershawn Palmer, thank your doing such a great job.

To Literary Divas, Moody Holiday, Electa Rome Park, Denise Turney, Joylynn Jossell, Desiree Dalton, Black Coffee, Diane Bromfield, and the Ladies of O.O.S.A , thank you for your contribution and insights without which this book wouldn't be the same.

To Andrew Morrison and all the members of the Book in 30 FaceBook Group, your support and information helped make this dream into a reality.

To my business coach, Monikah Orgando, for never taking my "buts" for an answer.

To all the members, past and present of Nubian Sistas Book Club, thank you for sharing your love of books with me.

Table of Contents

Preface 7

Introduction 9

Chapter 1 The Formation of Nubian Sistas Book Club 11

Chapter 2 Book Club Meeting Basics 13

Chapter 3 Go Tech 18

Chapter 4 Creating Book Tie-In Games 21

Chapter 5 Theme it Up 29

Chapter 6 Divas Night Out 31

Chapter 7 And Now the Book Discussion 32

Chapter 8 Invite an Author to Your Meeting 34

Chapter 9 Keep Them Coming Back For More 37

Chapter 10 Keys to a Fab Meeting 39

Resource Guide 41

Preface

A Literary Diva's Guide... was develop as part of a series of books and workshops geared to aid book club members in creating, hosting and maintaining a book club. In this book, you will find ways to organize a meeting, activities to include in your meeting, over 100 Book of the Month suggestions, resource guides, an agenda template and more. It is my hope that this book will be used as an integral tool by every book club looking for fun and innovative ways to start or enhance a club. For more information please visit www.thebookclubexpert.com

Are you a Literary Diva?

Would you like to be?

Join the **I'm a Literary Diva Book Club** for free at  www.imalitdiva.com. Once a member, you will have access to our weekly online discussions, our *Chat with an Author* bi-monthly tele-conference and receive our monthly *Between the Sheets* 'zine right to your door. You will also receive a chance to win free books, bookmarks, tote bags, and discounts on our Book of the Month selection as well as a 40% discount for our *I'm a Literary Diva Book Club Summit* held in Miami, Fl on September, 25th, 2010. Visit us online at www.imalitdiva.com for more information.

Introduction

A Brief History on African American Book Clubs

African American book clubs has been a part of our cultural for hundreds of years. Through book clubs and literary societies, men and particularly women have been able to express their thoughts and opinions with other likeminded individuals. Literary societies have been used as a mean to not only speak on racism but as an opportunity to share in the love of the written word as well. The history of book clubs is a powerful example of how African American has used their minds and not there fist to make changes in society.

In the years when Negros was considered inferior, educated group of colored members of societies began forming literary societies throughout the northern states. In 1827, the *Society of Young Ladies* was created in Lynn, Mass and became the first documented African American literary society, sparking the formation of other literary groups. According to the book, *We Are Your Sisters: Black Women in the Nineteen Century* the author, Dorothy Sterling, notes members hosted "mental feasts" which were meetings held for the purpose of educating themselves as well as to "combat white racism."

In September of 1931, *A Female Literary Society* held their first meeting which took place in Philadelphia. As the years went by more literary societies sprang up throughout the northern states with the purpose of educating themselves and to dispel the myth that all Negros were ignorant. As other literary societies were form, they became a means for many middle class, educated Colored women to meet and discuss literary articles, books, journals and poetry. Maybe the most significant of these groups were the *Society of Young Ladies* which help start several Colored women literary societies throughout the north. During these meetings or "mental feast", a member of the society would read a short address or literary piece to the group as well as hold discussions on slave trades, and the meeting usually ended with a hymn. African American reading groups have involved from such groups as *The Ladies Literary and Dorcas Society* which was form in the 1800s to

Oprah's Book Club which was started nationwide in 1996. The history of literary divas forming their own societies is an example of African Americans women using their words, thoughts and actions to create a means to express their views on society while sharing their love for knowledge and literature with like-minded individuals.

Today, African American book clubs are common place and many of our meeting practices are taken from the literary societies of the past. Thank to theses historical societies and past literary divas, we are able to enjoy the pleasure of being a part of a book club, today.

A Literary Diva can range from an author, a spoken word artist, a poet, an avid reader, to a book club president. Regardless of which category you fall under, we all have one thing in common; the love of the written word. For a history of the many African American women throughout our history that changed the way we view literature read *Literary Divas: The 100+ Most Admired African American Women in History by Heather Covington.* Learning about our literary history is essential to solidify your title as Literary Diva.

Chapter 1
The Formation of Nubian Sistas Book Club

More than likely, you purchased this book because you're either a member of a book club or plan to start one. Well, you made the right decision. *A Literary Diva's Guide to Starting a Fab Book Club Meeting* is a resource handbook for book club members looking for guidance in organizing or taking their meetings to the next level.

Book clubs have been a passion of mine since I formed Nubian Sistas Book Club in May of 2004. My goal for NSBC was to form a group of no more than 15 women who would exclusively read books either written by or primarily about an African American because I wanted to support and encourage the reading of African American books in my own small way.

Soon after starting the group, we expanded and grew to include services for authors by reviewing books. We formed *Review Divas: Nubian Sistas Book Review Team* and our website www.nubiansistas.org featured and promoted African American books as well as list literary events and workshops such as the Reading is a Pleasure literary series, which featured book readings from erotic authors, to our annual Literary Art and Culture Festival which included books reading from several AA authors, poets, dancers and singers. Because I have such a passion for promoting the reading of African American Books, in 2007 I formed Nubian Literary Network, a non-profit organization created to connect readers and authors while promoting African American literature within the community. Nubian Sistas Book Club and Nubian Literary Network have been fortunate to meet many authors including LA Banks, Shonda Cheekes and Trista Russell. We have also hosted several online chats with authors, Brandon Massey and others.

I started Nubian Sistas Book Club, Inc. on a whim. My cousin, Crystal and I, had just come from an empowerment seminar hosted by I.A.M., It's About Me, Inc. and the guest speaker was telling us a story of how she ended her career as a successful lawyer in order to pursue her passion as an author and guest speaker. As we drove home, Crystal and I talked about things we loved to do but for whatever reason never pursued. In the middle of the conversation, I blurted to her "Let's start a book club!" Crystal, who's game for nearly anything, agreed wholeheartedly and Nubian Sistas was born. But like all my ideas, I create the *concept* and worry about the *how* of it all afterwards. So, still on a high from my idea, I set a date, picked a book to discuss, mailed out fancy printed invites to all my book loving friends and family members in my age group, then sat back and said to myself, "Now what?"

I never hosted a book club before. Matter of fact, I had never been to a book club meeting. What do you do? What do you talk about? Who does what? After my initial panic, I did what I always did when faced with an overwhelming task; I Goggled. After days of combing the internet and printing out page after page of tips and suggestion from different online groups and How-To articles, I gathered all my resources and formed the basic concept for NSBC and created a format for our first meeting.

How did our first meeting go? It was ok. It was nice. However, the only memorable thing about it was the fact that it was our first meeting. Was it fab? No, not by a long shot but with each meeting I got better. I incorporated the activities that worked and got rid of the activities that didn't. As more members began hosting meetings, they too added their own spin to the discussions and before we knew it, our meetings became more engaging and fun. Soon we all looked forward to hosting and attending our meetings.

During my extensive Google searches, I remembered wishing that someone had written a book that would save me a ton of research time and provide me with the type of information I was looking for. Knowing that there was probably other literary divas out there facing the same problems, I decided to share some of the many activities and discussion formats NSBC has created or implemented. Remember, this is a reference guide not a This-Is-The-Only-Way-To-Do-It Guide. Take the tips and ideas in this book and put your own club's signature on it.

Chapter 2
The Basics of Book Club Meetings

When you start having your book club meetings, they will be one of the biggest highlights of your month. There's something about sitting down with a group of your girls while discussing a great book that is exhilarating. But what happens when you're a fresh book club and haven't created a methodology or the group has become bored with the same type of meeting, month in and month out? Well, shake things up of course. Think outside the box and you'll be surprised at how you can spice up your meeting or make your first book discussion amazing.

The Host with the Most

The first thing you need is a hostess/moderator. A meeting without a moderator can become disorganized and chaotic very quickly, especially when you're dealing with a club full of literary divas who have strong opinions about the Book of the Month (BOTM). Therefore, a moderator is highly recommended. How to assign hostess duties is up to you. Whether you decide to rotate duties from member to member, or draw names, your club should come up with a method that works for everyone. Regardless of how you decide to choose, picking a hostess may become one of the trickiest parts of the book meeting. You may have members who don't feel comfortable hosting the meeting or for whatever reason flat out refuse to share duties. Other divas may take offense and before you know it, there is a quiet (or maybe not so quiet) tiff going on among the members of the club. The best solution is to quickly implement a plan as soon as possible.

Diva Tip: Pre-pick an alternative host in case you have an emergency and can't make the meeting. Keep her abreast of the agenda you planned for the meeting so she can take over your duties seamlessly.

Also remind everyone that if any little disagreements arise they should be handled with diva like class.

Some tips for selecting a moderator are:

- Pull out your calendars and have members pick which month they would like to host
- Whoever suggests the next book of the month should host that particular meeting
- Select the next host during each meeting wrap-up
- Break up hosting duty into three month increments

Location, Location, Location

Surprising enough, the location of your meeting can have an overwhelming influence on a successful book discussion. For example, if you decide to have a meeting in a noisy restaurant where you have to speak loudly for everyone to hear you clearly, it might not be the best time to discuss a deep, dark, and intimate novel like, *PUSH* by Sapphire. Some location suggestions include: your home, park, book store, library, conference rooms and restaurants. Having a meeting in a conference room may seem unusual but like most of the tips in this book, NSBC has done it with great success. If you have a member who has weekend access to her office and can bring in guests, without worrying about getting fired, you should try hosting a meeting there.

> "We always meet in nice restaurants each month because we feel that at least once a month we should treat ourselves to a great meal. We always order our meals and socialize as we're eating. This gives us time to catch up with each other and discuss anything that we need to regarding the book club. We then discuss the book after we've eaten and taken care of our tab. This allows us to not have any interruptions and also if a member would like to join in on the discussion only, they have a specific time to meet up with us and not have to wait around. This seems to work well with my book club."
>
> TaNisha Webb
> KC Girlfriends
> Book Club President

Book stores are *EXTREMELY* book club friendly. Call your favorite book store and ask to speak to the manager or event coordinator and ask them if you can host a meeting there. Keep in mind, that some stores may add your meeting to their event calendars and open the meeting to the public. If you would like to keep it a closed meeting, ask them their policy before finalizing the details. Also, ask the manager when the best time or day is to hold a meeting, preferably when the store may expect the least amount of traffic.

Restaurants are a great way to meet with your literary divas in a relaxing environment without you, as the hostess, putting a lot of work in the planning of the food or entertainment.

Creating an Agenda

Book club meetings are usually run in one of two ways. I've labeled them as free rein and organized formats. In a free rein meeting, there is no set structure, conversations ebb and flow throughout the meeting and there is no set time or schedule.

In general, these types of meetings are easier to host. In a free rein meeting the book is discussed but the conversation flows in such a way that it doesn't feel like a meeting but more like a group of friends hanging out.

Free-rein meetings are perfect in restaurants since having games or discussing major club events don't work as well in public setting because it can be noisy (or too quiet to have a lively discussion) and may affect your planned meeting agenda.

With an organized format, you create a preset agenda and go through the outline step by step while keeping some form of structure throughout the meeting. This type of meeting works best for large groups, chat-rooms and teleconferences (chat-rooms and teleconferences are discussed later in this book).

Nubian Sistas has both meetings interchangeably, so feel free to switch it up and see which one works best for your group.

> *Diva Tip: If you see that everyone is either too excited about the book, only one other person read the book or everyone brought their kids and turned your home into a mini daycare, don't worry. Remember, meetings are supposed to be enjoyable, so just relax and go with the flow*

Meeting Agenda for *Man-Eater* by Mary B. Morrison and Noire

I.   Welcome/Refreshments

II.   Book Club Updates/Topic of discussion (this could be book members' news, planned outings, updating contact list etc…)

III.   *Puanny Island Scavenger Hunt*: (In the novel, Puny Island is an exclusive resort for women who are catered sexually by men)The host sets up a scavenger hunt using cut outs of different pictures from magazines, newsletters and printed clip art, including island and beach theme images. Create a list of images you would like the members to find (i.e. sandy beach, sunglasses, coconut drinks) and ask members to search through the box for the images. The person who finds the most items wins.

VI.   Book Discussion Questions

VII.   Next Month BOTM selection

VII.   Next host/location/date/time

VIII.   Meeting Overview and Wrap-up

Chapter 3
Go Tech

With the constant expanding world of technology, book clubs are no longer limited to live meetings. There are now several ways you can host your meeting to help accommodate the busy literary diva.

Online Chartroom

You don't need your own website or be a web designer to have a chartroom. Sites such as www.wireclub.com and www.buzzen.com have free services for anyone who would like to host a chat online; many rooms can be listed as private. Also, feel free to use the chartroom available at www.nubianliterarynetworkcom to host your online meetings.

Teleconference

Through the power of technology, literary divas are no longer limited in the way they hold a meeting. With the thousands of free apps and websites available to the public, you can expand your meetings in several different ways.

For example, if you're a diva on the go, a phone conference may be for you. Setting up an account on sites such as www.freephoneconference.com is easy. All you need is an email address. Once you receive a call-in phone number and pin number, simply email or text the information to your members along with meeting date and time. Before the meeting begins, call the number given to you a few minutes prior to the scheduled meeting time so you can greet the early birds. Once everyone arrives set some simple ground rules before starting the discussion. A major problem with phone conference is members can get distracted very easily and may start talking all at once. It's your job as head diva to keep everyone on topic so the meeting will run more smoothly and within the time frame.

Skype It

One of your literary divas can't make a meeting? Have them Skype in and they won't miss a thing. As long as you both have a laptop with a webcam and internet access, they can join the meeting while at home with a sick child or on a business trip. You can download Skype at www.skype.com. All Skype to Skype calls, video conference and teleconferences are free.

Social Networking and Blogs

Create an online presence for your club by starting a social network and/or blog. Most sites like www.wordpress.com or www.blogger.com offers free blogs and a variety of templates for you to use. By creating a site for your club, your members will have access to club information, updates on meeting and the latest BOTM with just a click of their mouse.

Incorporate video conferencing, chat rooms and twitter feeds into your site to make your social network more interactive. Many networks have

Diva Tip: Skype, Chat-rooms, and phone conferences can be used simultaneously. For example, if you are on a phone conference discussing a trip to the I'm a Literary Diva Book Club Summit, everyone can visit the website, imalitdiva.com, while on the call and discussing the different workshops you would like to attend.

privacy features which allow you to keep your information private. Nubian Sistas, for example, have a twitter account (www.twitter.com/nubianliterary) and a social network on ning.com (www.ning.com/nubiansistas). I set the privacy setting to "By Invite Only" and only members of the club have access to the site. Our site has our BOTM posted, our next book club date and location featured in the calendar and ongoing discussions posted in our forums. You can also use social networks like www.facebookcom and www.myspace.com to help spread the word about your book club and share information with other online book clubs.

As you can see, there is no one way to have a meeting, so go ahead, mix it up and have a little fun with the various ways of participating in your book club.

Chapter 4
Creating Book Tie-In Games

For NSBC, the most fun part of our meeting is
our games. What started as an icebreaker in
our first meeting became a must for each
discussion. From crossword puzzles to quizzes
we have tried to come up with different types
of games on a regular basis. If you're not
doing games at your meeting, you should
seriously consider it. It's a great way to make
your meeting more interactive and enjoyable
for all.

Finding ways to incorporate a game and basing
it on a book you're reading can be challenging,
but if you're stumped for ideas and don't like
the games in this guide, you can do research
online for icebreakers and adapt them to tie in
to the book. I have included a few games you
could use during your meeting to help expand
the book topic while making your members
smile. Anybody who has ever hosted a baby
shower probably has a step up in the game-tie in part of the meeting.
Below is a general list of games and icebreakers. At the end of some
game descriptions are specific games I already tied into a book which
you can use at your next meeting.

"With my group, I have created various ways for group members to get involved and be a part of the process. But … with (every) activity comes the behind the scenes work that make it all look like it runs itself. It takes time and love to keep it all going smoothly. If I have created some type of ongoing activity you can be sure that I have created some type of document to answer all questions. I am constantly looking for ways to make it run better and I am working on the next activity to keep the group and website running."

Desiree Dalton,
Founder/President
Sexy Ebony BBW
African American
Book Club

Dress Contests

When we read *The Hustler's Wife*, we had a ghetto-fab costume
contest and the person who had the best costume won (and no I didn't
win. My sister took that award). It was one of our most fun meetings.

<u>Cross Word Puzzle</u>

The easiest game to include in a meeting is, drum roll please…, crossword puzzles. There are several sites such as www.edhelper.com/crossword_free.htm, www.crosswordpuzzlegames.com and my personal favorite, www.puzzlemaker.discoveryeducation.com that have easy to fill out templates you can use to create a crossword puzzle, cryptograms and letter tiles.

On the next page is a crossword puzzle I created on puzzlemaker.discoveryeducation.com for the novel, *One Night with You* by Francis Ray. Please feel free to copy the puzzle and pass it out to your members at your next meeting.

***One Night with You* by Francis Ray**

J J V J H M A E A W W M L H N
A X I K A P X F M D C S F I Y
Z L X N Q N S O E B Q K A X N
S I C N A R F W R F S W D I I
E Z R C A L B I I F U R G O A
C G N K K M D B C E Y H V Y F
W U E R M E A O A L T N A K D
D R Y L Z B D N N B R R I X K
H P H E L W J H F U L A T H W
N R P X Z O M O Y O G B N E N
N A T I V E C J Z D T X H C C
P V O N O R A Q R G X J R O H
Y E L N W C L T W T P P H D E
E N E I E V A G I H J I E S P
H J H J S S E B F H L H R Q P

Word Search
AMERICAN
BLAC
COLLEGE
DOUBLE
DUNCAN
FRANCIS
JEEP
JOHN
MCBRIDE
NATIVE
NIGHT
ONE
PHD
RANCH
RAVEN
RAY

<u>Book Scavenger Hunt</u>

The moderator pulls several major events (like when a character found out she was pregnant or when she first met prince charming) from throughout the book and have the members find the chapters and pages these events took place. Keep it to about 3-5 events. You could also have it timed.

Book Scavenger Hunt for "Gimme an O" by Kayla Perrin

How did Dr, Lecia Calhoun and Anthony "T" Beals meet?
Answer: On *The Tonight Show with Jay Leno* (found between pages 23-33 in the book)

Which shoe company endorses Anthony?
Answer: *Nike* (pg 104)

When did Anthony start to believe that Ginger was really missing?
Answer: When he entered their home and notice her bags spewed across the floor and her wallet still in one of her bags (pgs 149-151)

<u>Book Quiz</u>

Create a quiz based on the book by creating about 7-12 questions and passing the printed quiz to your members. You can have it timed if you like and the person with the most answers wins.

Book Quiz for "Irresistible Forces" by Brenda Jackson
   1. What type of firm/business did Taylor Steele start?
       Answer: A wealth and asset management firm called *Assets of Steele*
   2. Who did she decide would be the father of her first child?
       Answer: Dominic Saxon
   3. What is the name of Dominic's driver
       Answer: Ryder
   4. What are the names of Taylor's sisters?
       Answer: Vanessa and Cheyanne
   5. How old was Dominic when someone attempted to kidnap him?
       Answer: Fourteen
   6. What kind of agreement did Dominic and Taylor agree in regards to custody of their possible child?
       Answer: They agreed on having joint custody of the child.
   7. What's the name of the island Dominic takes Taylor to?
       Answer: The island of Latios

<u>Text and Twitter Quiz</u>

To encourage everyone to read the book throughout the month, everyday, I would text the members with a book question and give a small prize to the first person who replies back with the correct answer. You can also use twitter to send out questions to your club.

For example, text and twitter questions for *This Fire Down in my Soul* by J.D. Mason could include "What's the name of the bar where Elise and Jay met?" (Answer: *Fred's*) or "What is Tess full first name?" (Answer: Contessa)

Prizes can range from the silly, like a pack of post-its to the more serious like a free copy of the next book of the month and free appetizers at the next meeting held in a restaurant.

I've noticed by texting questions to my club throughout the month, more members not only completed the book but finished the book well before the actual meeting.

Other games you can tie into a book are:

<u>20 questions</u>

Members try to guess the name of a character by asking you up to 20 questions about them.

<u>Two Truths and a Lie</u>

Each member take turns telling two truths and one lie about the book and everyone tries to guess which one is the lie. If they guess correctly the person who told the lie is out. Game continues until you have a winner.

<u>Character ID</u>

Each member receives a label with a book character name on it. The hostess helps place the label on their back without that member seeing the name on the label. As everyone mingles during the meeting, members ask each other "yes" or "no" question to receive clues on their

character. Towards the end of the meeting, ask each member which
character they think they are.

<u>M&Ms and You</u>

Pour some M&Ms into a candy bowl. Ask everyone to grab a
handful of M&Ms, but let them know they can't eat the candy just yet.
For each M&M they have in their hand they must answer a question
about themselves, the group, or about the BOTM.

Some suggestions include:

- Red candy: favorite character in book
- Green candy: favorite book ever read
- Yellow candy: most memorable book club meeting
- Orange candy: favorite place to read
- Brown candy: most embarrassing moments
- Blue candy: wild cards (another member can ask them a question)

<u>Paper Strip Story</u>

Cut out strips of paper and pass them, along with pens, out to
your members. Everyone then briefly writes down a true story or bizarre
experiences in no more than 3 sentences and write their name on the
bottom of the paper. Have them fold the strip of paper in half and put
them in a bowl. Shuffle the paper strips around and then randomly pick 4
pieces of paper. Read the names out loud of the 4 people and ask them to
in chairs or a couch apart from everyone else. Reads their stories and
then ask the remaining members to guess which stories belong to whom.
Once everyone connects the correct story to the correct person, repeat the
process till all the stories has been read and everyone had a chance to
participate.

<u>Hot Seat</u>

Assign a seat, or spot on the couch, as the "Hot Seat." Each member
takes turn sitting in the seat between 1-3 minutes. Members of the club
fires questions to the person sitting in the "hot seat" at rapid succession
but that person have the option to pass on any question they feel is too
personal. Members should ask meaningful questions that will help them

get to know their fellow club members better. Some suggested questions include:

- Which male book character would you love to date?
- Which author would you like some one-one time with?
- If you could change your career and be anything, what would it be?
- If you could change your name, what would you change it to?
- If you had Oprah's money, what would you do with it?
- What was your most embarrassing thing you ever got caught doing?
- What is the silliest thing you ever did?

<u>90 Day Vision Boards</u>

Ask your members to bring old magazines and a poster board to the next meeting and have glue sticks, markers, scissors and construction papers available to them. At the meeting, go around the room and ask each member what visions they have for themselves in the next 30, 60 and 90 days. After everyone talk about their goals, ask everyone to search the magazines for pictures and words that represent their goals and then glue it to their poster board. Have each member take the boards home but ask them to bring it back to the next two meetings so you can discuss the goals they're concentrating on. Use this activity as an opportunity to encourage and motivate each other. Make this an on-going activity and discuss the overall result at the end of the three months.

Chapter 5
Theme It Up

Having a theme for the meeting is FUN, FUN, FUN. There is an endless variety of ways to incorporate a theme into the book. Imagine reading *Flyy Girl* by Omar Tyree and at your meeting, dressing up in 80s gear, listening to 80s hip hop music and at the end of the discussion handing out Now and Laters and Blow Pops treat bags. Or reading *Man-Eater* by Mary B Morrison and Noire or *How Stella Got Her Groove Back* by Terry McMillan and having a tropical island theme with drinks out of coconut cups and wearing sarongs. Or reading *Waiting to Exhale* and then watching the movie during the meeting while sipping on champagne and jumping up and dancing when the girls in the movie start dancing.

You can also plan the food you have at the meeting around the book by simply changing the recipe name, for instance, renaming your chicken recipe to Chicken a la Joy King after the author of *A Dirty Little Secret*. Below are a few theme ideas I created to tie in with a book; but as always use your imagination and you'll be surprised with what you can come up with.

If you're reading:
an urban book like *The Cartel* 2 by Ashley and Jaquavis, *The Coldest Winter Ever* by Sister Souljah *or All That I Got is You* by The,oc…
Dress up in urban inspired clothing, create a playlist that includes Jay Z, Lil Wayne and Young Jeezy and have a bottle of Nuvo available on ice. For your hors d'oeuvres keep it simple like small chicken wings, strawberry and crème and meatballs.

romance books like *One Night with You* by Francis Ray or *Bachelor Untamed* by Brenda Jackson…
Have a Sunday brunch, with mimosa, croissants, creamy scrambled eggs, fruit salad, and Belgium waffles,

a memoir like *In Black in White* by LT Woody or *Finding* Fish by Antwone Fisher…
Keep the meeting intimate. Have some lattés, muffins, and cookies available and have the meeting in a cozy living room where you can sit and talk about, not only the book, but delve into some of your own emotions the book brought out of you.

Chapter 6
Divas Night Out

In between meetings, organize a night on the town for your club. Leave the book discussions for another time and enjoy some girl time. You'll enjoy hanging out with your club and will strengthen your bond as you while explore

your city or even take a trip together. Nubian Sistas has gone to New York for the Harlem Book Fair as well as Mexico and Jamaica for a little R and R. Spending time with your club will make your meetings more enriching as you discuss previous outings and plan new ones.

Diva Outing Suggestions

Day at the Spa

Museum

Poetry Readings

Book Fairs

Trips to another Country

A Day Cruise

Take a Gym Class Together

Host a Game-Board Night

A Day at a Country Club

Take a Pole Dancing Lesson (yes…pole dancing)

Go to a Gala Event

Host a Slumber Party

Go Bowling

Have a Chick-Flick Movie Night

Go Clubbing

Get Manicures and Pedicures together

Go out for Cocktails

Go on a Shopping Spree or go Window Shopping

Chapter 7
And Now the Book Discussion

You're sitting in your living room with your fellow divas, sipping on mimosa and nibbling on croissants. You just finish catching up with everyone when everyone turns to you ready to

"After we discuss the book, we go around in the circle and will tell each sista what is fabulous about each other. The sista who is receiving the acknowledgement must take a moment to receive then we move to the next person. This is a great exercise because many times there isn't any one to give us validation and sometimes other sisters are known for tearing each other down. So we are working on trusting our sistas again and reclaiming that sisterhood that we once had."

Diana Bromfield,
Book Club Member
W.I.S.E. Book Club

discuss the book. A book discussion is just that, a discussion of what you read, what you thought of the plot, the characters and the writing style of the author. There are several books published right now that include book discussion questions in the back, but not all books have them. So you're faced with the task of creating your own questions. Ok, don't panic. Take a deep breath. It's not as hard as you think. Remember you are a literary diva and can come up with book discussion questions in your sleep.

When creating your questions remember the Who, What, When, Where, Why and How of the book. Asking questions that only require one word answers will only limit your discussion. Questions could be written around how they liked the book, what they got from it and what impression did it leave with them.

Included in reference section of this book is a list of novels and non-fiction books that I've compiled with the help of various AA authors and book clubs to (I love my self-published authors) to better aid your book discussion. The reference section has a list of BOTM sorted by genre and also includes a few reading guides for you. For those that would like to create their own questions, I've included a generic list of discussion questions that you can customize to fit most books. But your biggest resource is your members. Ask them to come up with one to three questions and either takes turns asking them or writes them down beforehand, and give them to you to share with the group.

Remember the key to a fab meeting in the end is the actual book club discussion. Keep your members engaged, ask a mix of deep, meaningful, funny, and rhetorical questions and stay away from one word answers. And to help keep the conversation going make sure to ask in your questions: Why or Why Not?

<u>Generic Book Discussion Questions</u>
1) What was the underlying theme in the novel?
2) What was your favorite part of the book?
3) Who was your favorite character? Why?
4) Which character was your least favorite? Why?
5) What part of the story stuck out to you the most?
6) Did you relate to the main character? Why or Why Not?
7) Would you read another book written by this author? Why or why not?
8) Have you ever been in this type of situation yourself? Explain.
9) Would you recommend this book to someone else? Why or Why Not?
10) Do you think this book can be turned into a movie? If so, which actors would you like to see play the main characters in the film?

Chapter 8
Inviting an Author to Your Meeting

Many authors are thrilled to attend a book club meeting. They enjoy interacting with members and the one on one feedback they receive about their book is priceless. But many book clubs don't reach out to authors because they don't know how, are afraid to ask or don't know how to find them.

Nubian Sistas first book club meeting with an author was with Shonda Cheekes author of *Another Man's Wife* and we were so nervous. We loved her book so much, we became awestruck and wasn't sure what to do, what to say or how to act. Our meeting that day was at *Bahamas Breeze* in Pembroke Pines, Fl and as we sat down and started talk to her you could sense a collective sigh of relief when we all realized that she was just like us. She loved books, she talked about different authors, and she kept track with the literary community just like we did. She was truly a literary diva.

What you need to keep in mind is that authors are people just like you. The only difference between them and you is that they put their thoughts into printed words and decided to share it with the world.

So, how can you start inviting authors to your meeting? First, seek out local authors. Local authors are easy to reach out too because they live in your own back yard. A great way to connect to African American (AA) authors is through social networks like Nubian Literary Network which has a nice mix of authors and members interacting and networking with each other. Our website is www.nubianliterarynetwork.com. Go ahead and post a message in the forum room and ask if there's any authors that lives in the area that would like to attend a meeting.

You can also contact various authors directly on through their website and through there publishing companies. I've included a list of authors in the resource section of the book but you can also visit websites like www.blackrefers.com and www.aalbc.com for a more through list of AA authors and their sites. For those authors who would like to attend your meeting but can't make it personally, now would be a great time to set up a teleconference or Skype the author into your meeting. Once you find an author work out an agreeable time to have your meeting.

Now, listen to me my divas, this is not the month to share one book among ten members. Support the author and show them how much you appreciate them by having each member buy a book. Also, since I'm still on my soapbox, let me share with you a little insight. Authors put their blood, sweat, and sometimes a lot of tears into writing a book. There's a long process of getting a book publish starting from finding an agent and getting an publishing company's acceptance letter, to going through the editorial process and finally having that book printed.

Then you have those authors that self publish their book and pour their own money into making their dream into a reality. Now that being said, when your club is sitting around talking to an author or attending a book signing please refrain from telling them you bought their book and loved it so much you shared it with Ray-Ray, Junebug, Taneisha, and them. We all share books with our friends, it's a given. But we inform the author that at every opportunity possible.

Considering all the time, money, and effort that go into each book printed, the best way to support your favorite author is by spreading the word about how good their book is and suggesting to your friends and

> "The president should send an email to introduce the book club's interest in the author's work and then simply ask. Most authors are pleased to have their work read by a book club.
> Don't be afraid to have a phone meeting with the author if there is considerable distance involved. Also use this as a backup if weather or travel delays prevent a personal appearance."
> Moody Holiday,
> Author of *The Black Divorce*

family members they should buy it. Ok, I'm getting off my soapbox now and tucking it away for future use.

Chapter 9
Keep Them Coming Back For More
The three main problems many book clubs face are:
1.   Member not attending meetings
2.   Members not reading the BOTM
3.   Members dropping out of the club

NSBC have faced these problems countless times and the best way to handle it is by catering to the members who really want to be in your club and letting the ones who don't show a true interest in the group, part ways so you can make room for a more active new member. Book club has its influx of membership and that natural. But here are some ways to keep your membership levels up and keep your members interested in coming back for more.

To encourage them to read the book of the month
1.   Hold a text/twitter contest:
They really get excited to see what questions you will send them each day.
2.   Assign Homework: Break down the book into pages or chapters and assign them certain pages to read each week.
3.   Hold a contest for the person who finishes the book first.

To Encourage Them to Attend Meetings
1. Hold a contest where the person who arrive first wears a tiara during the whole meeting and is the Queen Diva of the day
2. Have gift baskets prepare for the first couple of members that arrive on time
3. Tell them you have a surprise for everyone who arrive and give them a simple gift like identical notepads and pens they can use to jot down notes for their next meeting.

If you lost a lot of members who recently drop out of your book club
1. Ask current members in your club to recruit their co-workers, family members and friends, and ask them to sit in on your next meeting and possibly join the club.

2. Hold a membership drive at your local library or book store by having a meeting available to the public or post your next meeting at www.meetup.com.

Chapter 10

Keys to a Fab Book Club Meeting

Book clubs are great ways to expand your circle of friends, meet new people and to interact with those who enjoys book just as much as you do. It's also the perfect way for you to expand your book knowledge and sample books in a variety of genres. Through book clubs, we have the opportunity every month to discuss our passion with others and gaining new insights and points of views from other people.

Book clubs are a part of our cultural background and an integral part of our community. By joining, or starting a club you are becoming a part of our literary history and paving the way for future generations. Start sharing your passion for books with other young, up and coming literary divas and they will continue to add to our literary tapestry and begin connecting with other book clubs online.

Keep your book club meeting fun and make your book club unique from the rest. The only thing that limits your book club and your meetings is your imagination. By using some of the ideas I gave you in this book, you'll be surprised at how soon you will become inspired and start creating your own activities. Hosting a book club is enjoyable and for every literary diva, a pleasure to attend each month.

Remember these actions:

1. Create a process for selecting a hostess
2. Choose a location keeping the overall type of meeting you want to have in mind.
3. Create an agenda that includes book discussions questions, book club items to be discussed and activities
4. Incorporate technology into your book club and meetings.
5. Use Book Tie-In Games to liven up your meeting

So when planning, remember to be creative, be inspired, be inventive and you will start hosting the most fab book club meetings ever.

Please let me know how your meetings turn out by emailing me at nubianlit@gmail.com. I would love to hear about your book club, any stories you would like to share and any games you invented.

Also if you would like to receive our monthly 'zine, *Between the Sheets*, which features the latest and greatest in African American literature or would like to network with other book clubs and authors please visit www.nubianlit.com. You can also join our book club at www.imalitdiva.com. Also, please visit my blog at www.thebookclubexpert.com.

Resource Guide

Teleconference

Skype

www.skype.com

FreeConferenceCall.com

www.freeconferencecall.com

No Cost Conference

www.nocostconference.com

Instant Conference

www.instantconference.com

Chat Rooms

WireClub

www.wireclub.com

Nubian Literary Network

www.nubianliterarynetwork.com

TinyChat

www.tinychat.com

Video Conferencing

Skype

www.skype.com

Oovoo

www.oovoo.com

Palbee

www.palbee.com

Social Networks

Twitter

www.twitter.com

Facebook.com

www.facebook.com

MySpace

www.myspace.com

Ning

www.ning.com

Social Go

www.socialgo.com

- Adam Mansbach www.adammansbach.com/
- Aisha Ford www.aishaford.com/
- Alice Holman www.aliceholman.com
- Allison Hobbs www.allisonhobbs.com
- Alonda Alloway www.authorsden.com/alondaalloway
- Tanya Bates www.tanyabates.com
- Andrea Blackstone www.dreamweaverpress.net/home.htm
- Baba Evans www.authorsden.com/babaevans
- Barbara Custer www.bloodredshadows.com
- Brandon Massey www.brandonmassey.com
- Brenda Jackson www.brendajackson.net
- C. Kelly Robinson www.ckellyrobinson.com
- Carl Weber www.carlweber.net
- Cassandra Bell www.cassandrabell.com
- Charlotte Russell Johnson www.reachingbeyond.net
- Cheryl Robinson www.cherylrobinson.com
- Claudia Brown Mosley www.claudiabrownmosley.com
- Cydney Rax www.booksbycydney.com
- Darnella Ford www.darnella.com
- Denise Turney www.chistell.com
- Donna Hill www.donnahill.com
- Electa Rome Parks electaromeparks.blogspot.com
- E. Lynn Harris www.elynnharris.com
- Eric Jerome Dickey www.ericjeromedickey.com
- Eric Pete www.ericpete.com
- Francine Yates www.franyates.net
- Gloria Mallette www.gloriamallette.com
- Gwynne Forster www.gwynneforster.com
- Joy C. Farrington www.thebookclubexpert.com
- JM Jeffries jmjeffries.com
- Karen E. Quinones-Miller www.karenequinonesmiller.com
- Karrine Steffans www.karrine.com

- Kayla Perrin www.kaylaperrin.com
- Kim Robinson
  www.kim-robinson.com
- L.A. Banks www.vampirehuntress.com
- Lexi Davis www.lexidavis.com
- Linda Dominique Grovenor www.lindadominiquegrovenor.com
- Moody Holiday www.moodyholiday
- Noire www.asknoire.com
- Omar Tyree www.ormartyree.com
- Relentless Aaron www.relentlessaaron.com
- Rochelle Alers www.rochellealers.com
- Sandra Kitt www.sandrakitt.com
- TL James www.authortljames.com
- Toure www.toure.com
- Victor McGlothin www.victormcglothin.com
- Vincent Alexandria www.victoralexandria.com
- Virgina Deberry www.deberryandgrant.com
- Yasmin Shiraz www.yasminshiraz.net
- Yolanda Joe www.yolandajoe.com
- Zane www.streborbooks.com
- Zekita www.zeniampublications.com

Top Ten Online Book Club

- ➤ African American on the Move Book Club
  www.aambookclub.com
- ➤ African American Literature Book Club
  www.aalbc.com
- ➤ APOOO (A Place of Our Own)
  www.apooobooks.com
- ➤ Go On Girl Book Club
  www.goongirl.org
- ➤ The Grits
  www.thegrits.com
- ➤ KC Girlfriends Book Club
  www.kcgirlfriendsbookclub.com
- ➤ OOSA Online Book Club
  www.oosa.com
- ➤ RAWSISTAZ Literary Group
  www.rawsistaz.com
  Sexy Ebony BBW African American Book Club
  www.sexyebonybbwaabookclub.com
- ➤ SistahFriend Book Club
  www.sistahfriend.com
- ➤ Street Gangs' Book Club
  www.streetgangs.com/bookclub

Top Ten Local Chapters

- The Imani Book Club, Montgomery, AL
  www.imanivoices.com
- Club Mimosa Book Club, Harrisburg, PA
  www.clubmimosabookclub.com
- Powerful Women of Praise Book Club, Inland
  Empire, CA www.powerfulwomenofpraise.com
- Sisters That Are Reading (S.T.A.R.), Westchester,
  NY

  prositesreading01.homestead.com
- The Little Black Book Club, Miami, Fl
  www.thelittleblackbookclub.com/
- Sistahfriend Book Club, Chapters in SC, NC, GA,
  TN, LA, www.sistahfriendbookclub.com
- Bonded Through Books Cleveland, OH
  www.bondedthroughbooks.com
- ASiS Book Club, Washington, DC
  www.asisbookclub.org
- Sisters and Brothers of Hotlanta Literary Club,
  Atlanta GA
  www.sistersandbrothersofhotlanta.com
- The Pearls Book Club, Baltimore, MD
  www.thepearlsbook.club.com

*Meeting
Supplements*

(name of book club)

Book Club Meeting

Date: **Time:** **Location:**
Moderator: **Notes Taker:**
Attendances:
Book for Discussion:
Agenda Items

Topics:
    ➤
    ➤
    ➤
    ➤
    ➤
    ➤
    ➤
    ➤

Activities:

>
>
>

Book Discussion Questions

1.
2.
3.
4.
5.
6.
7.
8.
9.
10.
11.
12.
13.
14.
15.

Special Notes/ Meeting Wrap-up:

>
>
>
>
>
>

Urban/Erotica

- *Flyy Girl* by Omar Tyree
- *The Coldest Winter Ever* by Sistah Soulja
- *A Hustler's Wife* by Nikkie Turner
- *Gangsta* by K'wan
- *Dopefiend* by Donald Goines
- *True to the Game* by Teri Woods
- *G-Spot* by Noire
- *Bitch* by Dejah King
- *Thug-a-licious* by Noire
- *Addicted* by Zane
- *All I Got is You* by The,oc
- *The Black Divorce* by Moody Holiday
- *Wild Innocence* by Moody Holiday
- *Heart Breaker by* Denesha Diamond, Erick S. Gray and Nichelle Waller
- *Dirtier than Ever* by Vicki M. Stringer
- *One Dead Preacher* by Tony Lindsay
- *Chocolate Covered Forbidden Fruit* by Trista Russell
- *Fly on the Wall* by Trista Russell
- *She's No Angel* by Janice A Morris
- *How Do You Want It* by Darnell King
- *A Rich Man's Baby* by Daaimah S. Poole
- *Tappin' on Thirty* by Candice Dow

Mainstream

- *The Twilight Saga* by Stephanie Meyers
- *The Lost Symbol* by Dan Brown
- *The Davinci Code* by Dan Brown
- *The Girl with the Dragon Tattoo* by Steig Larson
- *The Shack* by William P. Young
- *I, Alex Cross* by James Patterson
- *Under the Dome* by Stephen King
- *Sookie Stackhouse Series (True Blood)* by Charlene Harris
- *The Last Song* by Nicholas Sparks
- *Pirates Latitudes* by Stephen King
- *Olive Kitteridge* by Elizabeth Strout
- *The Lovely Bones* by Alice Sebold
- *The Hunger Games* by Suzanne Collins

Classics

- *The Color Purple* by Alice Walker
- *Their Eyes Were Watching God* by Zora Neale Hurston
- *Beloved* by Toni Morrison
- *Invisible Man* by Ralph Ellison
- *Disappearing Acts* by Terry McMillian
- *I Know Why the Caged Bird Sing* by Maya Angelou
- *Song of Solomon* by Toni Morrison
- *Native Son* by Richard Wright
- *A Raisin in the Son* by Lorraine Hansberry
- *Roots: The Saga of a American* Family by Alex Haley
- *The Miseducation of the Negro* by Carter G. Woodson
- *Make Me Wanna Holler* by Nathan McCall
- *Manchild in the Promise Land* by Claude Brown
- *A Lesson Before Dying* by Ernest Gaines
- *The Souls of Black Folks* by W.E.B. Dubois

Poetry

- *The Selected Poems of Nikki* Giovanni (1968-1995) by Nikki Giovanni
- *I Am the Darker Brother: An Anthology of Modern Poems by African Americans* by Arnold Adoff and Benny Andrews
- *Black Coffee: Poems to Get African American Women Though the Day* by Thomalyn A. Epps.
- *The Collected Poems of Langston Hugh* by Langston Hugh
- *The Moments, the Minutes, the Hours Poetry* by Jill Scott
- *The Vintage Book of African American Poetry* by Michael S. Harper and Anthony Walton
- *Soulscript: A Collection of Classic African American Poetry* by June Johnson
- *I, Too, Sing America: Three Centuries of African American Poetry* by Catherine Clinton and Stephen Alcorn
- *The Book of American Negro Poetry* by James Weldon Johnson

Non-Fiction

- *Finding Fish* by Antwone Fisher
- *The Autobiography of Malcolm X* by Malcolm X and Alex Haley
- *Make Me Want to Holler: A Young Black Man in America* by Nathan McCall
- *The Autobiography of an Ex-Colored Man* by James Weldon Johnson
- *Billy* by Albert French
- *Don't Let the Lipstick Fool You: The Making of a Champion* by Lisa Leslie
- *Act Like a Lady, Think Like a Man* by Steve Harvey
- *Black Like Me* by John Howard Griffin
- *Brother West: Living and Loving Out Loud* by Cornel West and David Ritz
- *The Measure of a Man* by Sidney Poiter
- *Dreams from my Father* by Barrack Obama
- *No Place Safe: A Family Memoir* by Kim Reid
- *A Piece of Cake, a Memoir* by Cupcake Brown

Young Adult (YA)

- *Boy Shopping* by Nia Stephens
- *Drama High Series* by L. Divine
- *Prime Choice Perry Sky Jr. Series* by Stephanie Perry Moore
- *Trouble Follows* by Monica Mckayhan
- *Can't Stop the Shine* by Joyce Davis
- *Pushing Pause* by Celest O. Norfleet
- *November Blues* by Sharon M. Drapers
- *Cooper Sun* by Sharon M. Drapers
- *When the Black Girl Sings* by Bill Wright
- Sounder
- *Shayla's Double Brown Baby Blues* by Lori Aurelua Williams

Thought-Provoking

- *Them* by Nathan McCall
- *Another Country* by James Baldwin
- *Tumbling* by Dianne McKinney-Whetstone
- *The Street* by Ann Petry
- *The Souls* of Black Folk by W.E.B. Dubois
- *Miss Ophelia* by Mary Burnett Smith
- *Push* by Sapphire
- *Race Matters by Cornel West*
- *Colored People: A Memoir* by Henry Louis Gates Jr.
- *The Audacity of Hope* by Barrack Obama
- *The Covenant in Action* by Travis Smiley and Cornel West
- *The Ways of White Folks* by Langston Hugh
- *Middle Passage* Charles Johnson
- *Debating Race with Michael Eric Dryson* by Michael Eric Dryson

Sci-fi, Fantasy and Horror

- *Kindred* by Octavia Butler
- *My Soul to Keep* by Tananarive Butler
- *The Between* by Tananarive Due
- *Blood Colony* by Tananarive Due
- *Shadow Valley* by Stephen Barnes
- *The Shadow Speaker* by Nnedi Okorafor Mbachu
- *Wind Follower* by Carole McDonnell
- *Cornered* by Brandon Massey
- *Dark Corner* by Brandon Massey
- *The Darker Mask* by Gary Phillipps
- *Imaro* by Charles Saunders
- *Vampire Huntress Legend Series* by L.A. Banks
- *Skin Folks* by Nalo Hopkins

Christian and Inspirational

- *The Prodigal Husband* by Jacqueline Thomas
- *Cruisin'* on Desperation by Pat G'orge Walker
- *One Prayer Away* by Kendra Norman-Bellamy
- *Boaz Brown* by Michelle Morrison
- *The Last Woman Standing* by Tia McCullurs
- *Illusions* by Wanda B. Campbell
- *Secrets of a Sinner* by Yolanda Tonnette Sanders
- *Temptation* by Victoria Christopher Murray
- *He's Fine... But is He Saved* by Kimberly Brooks
- *Forgiving Aint Forgettin*: *A Novel* by Marta Elliot
- *Have a Little Faith* by Reshonda Tate Billingsley
- *Be Careful What you Pray* For by Kimberla Lawson Roby
- *My Soul Cries Out by Sherri Lewis*
- *One Day by Soul Just Open Up* by Iyanla Vanzant
- *Sweet Bye-*Bye by Denise Michelle Harris
- *The Pastor's Wife by* Reshonda Tate Billingsley
- *Reposition Yourself* by T.D. Jakes
- *Secret Sisterhood* by Monique Miller
- *She Who Finds a Husband* by Joylynn Jossell

Fiction

- *Sins of the Father* by Angela Benson
- *Mama Dearest* by E. Lynn Harris
- *God Ain't Blind* by Mary Monroe
- *The Secret Life of Bees* by Sue Monk Kidd
- *Resurrecting Midnight* by Eric Jerome Dickey
- *His First Wife* by Grace Octavia
- *Counterfeit Wives* by Phillip Thomas Duck
- *Sinful Too* by Victor Mcglothin
- *Love, Lies, and Scandal* by Earl Sewell
- *She Had it Coming* by Mary Monroe
- *Sweet Georgia Brown* by Cheryl Robinson
- *Passin'* by Karen Quinones Miller
- *Big Girls Don't Cry* by Carl Webber
- *Uptown* by Virgina Deberry and Donna Grant
- *Little Black Girl Lost Series* by Keith Lee Johnson
- *A Long Walk Up by Denise Turney*
- *A Time to Learn by Black Coffee*
- *Diary of a Stalker* by Electa Rome Park

Name:

Address:
Phone Number:
Email Address:
Twitter Username:
Additional Information:

Name:

Address:
Phone Number:
Email Address:
Twitter Username:
Additional Information:

Name:

Address:
Phone Number:
Email Address:
Twitter Username:
Additional Information:

Name:

Address:
Phone Number:
Email Address:
Twitter Username:
Additional Information:

Diary of a Stalker by Electa Rome Park

Discussion Questions

1) Do you think groupies exist in the literary world?

2) Did Xavier take advantage of Pilar in the beginning of their relationship?

3) What are your feelings regarding Pilar? Did you like/dislike her? Feel sorry for her?

4) What are your feelings regarding Xavier? Did you like/dislike him? Do you know men like him?

5) Do you feel Xavier's womanizing ways were a by-product of his upbringing?

6) Why do you feel Xavier continued to sleep with Pilar *after* experiencing some of her irrational behavior?

7) Did Xavier get what he deserved? Why or why not?

8) Could Pilar have overcome her past?

9) Did Pilar learn anything by the end of the book? Did Xavier?

10) Have you ever been stalked? Have you ever stalked anyone?

11) In the electronic era, do you think excessive emailing is a form of stalking?

12) What about keeping up with someone from an online site such as myspace, facebook or twitter?

13) Had you figured out who Leeda was?

14) What was your favorite scene from Diary of a Stalker?

15) Do you feel Xavier has seen the last of Pilar?

Long Walk Up by Denise Turney

Discussion Questions

Q: What event awakens Mulukan to her destiny?

Discussion: Early in the story Mulukan is made to experience an event that psychologists note changes a person permanently. At six years old, Mulukan stands like a stranger amid people from the only community she has ever known. She watches her mother's burial as if she is simply watching a bird fly across the sky. Yet, the event, the unrecoverable event, stirs something deeply within Mulukan. The following morning she walks away from every shred of familiarity and sets out on a course only her heart and her inner spirit know the way upon.

Q: What role did Mulukan's other family members play in her life?

Discussion: Mulukan's father was a leader in the community. His courage and wisdom helped the people in the community (also referred to by journalists and historians as a tribe) to survive long months of drought. The few short years Mulukan spent observing, watching, her father taught her that leadership demands courage of its participants.

Q: Do hardships truly sharpen a person?

Discussion: Think about how blessed and emotionally uplifting experiences show up seemingly out of nowhere to be deposited into Mulukan's life the same way that hard and emotionally painful experiences show up for the little girl. What do you think would happen to Mulukan if these experiences were not balanced, if she had many more hard experiences than miraculously good experiences or vice versa? Would she be equipped to step inside her destiny?

Q: How can a child believe in eternity?

Discussion: Is it easier to believe that Mulukan's mother could readily identify and communicate with Mulukan than it is to believe that Mulukan could readily and fully identify her mother's spirit and communicate with her mother? What happens to illustrate that Mulukan is as much spirit as is her transitioned mother?

Q: Is it easy to miss one's destiny?
Discussion: Did Mulukan know who the key people in her life were when she first met them? Why or why not? Would her life have been different if she had known the role people like Desta and the truck driver would have in her life before or just as she met them? Why or why not?

Q: The remainder of her life.
Discussion: What became of Mulukan after she began to lead an African nation? Did she get married? If she did get married, what type of wife or mother do you think she was? If Mulukan had daughters and sons, what do you think their destinies were?

Q: Mulukan as a mother herself
Discussion: Lastly, do you think Mulukan would allow her children to discover their own destiny or do you think she would interfere in their lives and try to lead them on a specific path she thought they should journey upon? Why do you think this?

Discussion Questions

1) Although the subtitle of this book is "She Who Finds a Husband," it was evident that God's word is sovereign, which states "He who finds a husband..." Do you believe once the women let go and let God's word prevail by allowing their husbands/mates to find them, things turned out better?

2) Paige had a problem with one of her co-workers. She felt he ignored the fact that she was now a Christian, since he was used to dealing with the old, more worldly Paige. How do you feel a born again person should deal with those types of situations; be it co-workers, family or friends? Have you ever found yourself in a similar situation? If so, how did you deal with it and was it effective?

3) Deborah carried around guilt and shame because of an act she'd committed years ago that she regretted doing. Instead of confessing the act to God, she felt as though she was hiding it from Him, and then got angry with Helen for threatening to reveal it. Do you think that is what the accuser is doing to so many Christians today in order to keep them in bondage; in God's ear accusing, while all the time God is simply waiting on His child to confess the sin to Him directly so that healing and deliverance can begin?

4) Some of the women at New Day put on a church face and assumed Mother Doreen had been doing the same. Do you agree with Mother Doreen; that just because a person is going through something, they don't always have to appear broken? That an experience with the Lord and even the mere anticipation of a move of God can be magnified over the problem or situation itself?

5) Helen had committed the same act herself that she taunted Deborah about having committed. Do we as Christians sometimes try to justify or cover acts we've committed that might not have been pleasing to God by pointing our finger in the direction of someone who we feel did something even worse?

6) Because of Deborah's actions that day in Family Café, Zelda made a decision that she didn't want to attend New Day Temple of Faith. In real life, do you believe that the actions of the members of a church play a role in whether people decide to attend that church, or is a reflection on the kingdom as a whole?

7) Deborah blamed herself for ending up in the predicament she did with Elton. Do you agree, somewhat agree, or totally disagree that she was to blame?

8) Paige had allowed her mother's role in the marriage to her father to shape her thoughts on relationships. The last thing Paige wanted to do was to find a man that was like her father to avoid ending up like her mother. Do you think Paige might have missed out on a man God had for her because of her way of thinking?

9) There were a couple of unfortunate mishaps at New Day Temple of Faith regarding the use of the Internet. Do you believe the Internet can be used as a weapon of the enemy to attack Christians and mankind in general? How should we protect ourselves from the enemy's use of this form of technology?

10) Were Paige's issues that she needed to be delivered from less significant than those of some of the other characters' in the book? Why or why not?

11) Tamarra carried around loads of baggage from her past. Even though she seemed to be delivered from so much, there always seemed to be

even more issues she had to face. Have you ever felt that way? That you'll never be able to shed all the burdens laid upon you?

12) What biblical story can you relate Tamarra and her brother's situation to?

13) Which characters, whether main characters or background characters from She Who Finds a Husband would you like to see in future New Day Divas series?

14) Were there any particular characters, issues or situations that you could closely relate to?

15) Although Tamarra's mother didn't attend church or believe God to work in her own life, she always questioned Tamarra about church and God in hers. Why do you think that is so? Do you know non-Christians like that? Ones who won't allow God to operate in their own life, but keeps you under the Christian microscope?

Book Discussion Questions

1) How familiar were you with the generational oversight of elders, in African American relationships, before reading this book? Do you feel this extended family is drawing on its African culture with how they maintain order amongst the generations?

2) Did you believe that many marriages were arranged by elders, in African American families, before you read this book?

3) How did your impressions of the Cleveland crew shift throughout the book, from the very telling first chapter, Daddy's home, to the somber Jeremy's Trials or the seemingly heartless Hell-ava party and on to the gut wrenching final chapter, The
Way it is?

4) How does Ajay's treatment of Ebony affect your views of him?

5) How important is loyalty in a family? In a relationship?

6) How important is good and satisfying sex, in a relationship between a man and a woman? Should he put her needs first? Should she put his needs first?

7) Should a woman have an orgasm with each sexual experience? Should men be taught that sexual satisfaction is important for the woman, as well?

8) What is the average age of the crew girls when they first experience sex? Do you think this novel captures the reality of first sexual experiences? Do you think this novel covers the gap in experience between males and females in the wonder years to date or have females become the dominator?

9) At what age should a young man be taught the appropriate way to treat a young lady? At what age should a young lady be taught what to tolerate and expect from a young man?

10. Are relationship traits hereditary? Do you believe in a family cycle when it comes to how relationships are formed and how they turn out?

11) Before reading this novel, did you feel like all males prefer that they're wives be virgins to them?

12) What is your best example of the girl or boy next door?

13) Do you feel that the success of these couples, in Chill's crew, will be a testament to the Matrons and Matriarchs of the family or a disgrace?

     A. Do you think elders should advise their offspring about relationships?

     B. Should their advice be graphic and to the point or water down?

14) Breast Cancer and Diabetes are not prevalent in the black community. T or F

15) Of all the relationships and marriages in the entire crew, which one do you relate to best?

16) Which boy or girl, in the crew, is your ideal mate?

17) Which individual character reminds you of yourself?

18) What do you think will become of Chill's crew?

19) Will the death of one member, change the outlook for Chill's crew?

20) Does Ajay love Ebony? Will Ebony ever like Raymond White?

21) What do you think about Ajay's relationship to his father, Allen?

22) What common threads run through this novel and novels by other authors you've read?

23) What's the most memorable thing about Time to Learn?

24) Which direction do you think this series will go?

25) What would you most like to see in this series? Would you like to see this visualize on stage or in film?

Book Sellers

Alabama

**Black Classics
(Books & Gifts)**
2206 Airport
Blvd., Suite D
Mobile, AL 36606
(334) 476-1060
(334) 476-4642
FAX
Contact: Adline
Clarke

**Roots &Wings, A
Cultural
Bookplace**
1345 Carter Hill
Rd.
Montgomery, AL
36106-1421
(334) 262-1700
(334) 262-8498
(fax)
Contact: Gwen
Boyd

California

**The African
Book Mart**
2440 Durant Ave
Berkeley, CA

94704-1611
510-843-3088

**Aswad's
Bookstore**
www.bookmasters
.com/aswad
mraswad@aol.co
m
212-256-6000 ext
12360573

Books In Color
5444 Watt Avenue
North Highlands,
CA
(916) 334-2026
Contact: Sherri

**Bright Lights
Bookstore**
8461 S. Van Ness
Ave.
Inglewood, CA
90305
(213) 971-1296
(805) 583-0207
(fax)
Contact: Michael
McAllen

**Carol's Books
&Things**
5964 S. Land Park
Dr.
Sacramento, CA
95822
(916) 428-5611
Contact: Melba
McNeal-Whitaker

Eso Won Books
3655 S. La Brea
Ave.
Los Angeles, CA
90016
(213) 294-0324

**Hanna's Ethnic
Bookseller**
240 Blue
Mountain Way
Claremont, CA
91711-2825
(909) 626-5051
Contact: Carter A.
Hanna

**IronWood
Corner**
462 Toolen Place
Pasadena, CA.
91103

(818)398-5539
(818) 797-1097
(fax)
contact: Burma

Johari Books
2140 E. Palmdale
Blvd. Unit N"
Town Square
Shopping Center
Palmadale, CA
93550
(805) 538-1001
(805) 538-1919
(fax)

**Phenix
Information
Center**
381 N "E" Street
San Bernardino
Ca. 92401
909.383.2329 fax
909.383.2331
email:
phenix@dreamsof
t.com
Faron and Joann
Roberts, co-
owners
*Specialize in
African American
Literature and
Entertainment*

**Zahra's
Books~N~Things**
900 N. La Brea
Ave.
Ingelwood, CA
90302
310-330-1300
Mon - Sat 10am to
7pm
Sunday 12noon -
5pm

Canada

**A Different
Booklist**
746 Bathurst St.
Toronto, Canada
(416) 538-0889
Contact: Wesley
Crichlow

Colorado

Black And Read
7821 Wadsworth
Blvd
Arvada, CO
80003-2107
303-467-3236

**Hue-Man
Experience**
911 Park Ave. W.

Denver, CO 80205
(303) 293-2665
(303) 293-0046
(fax)
Contact: Clara
Villarosa

Connecticut

**Black Books
Galore, Inc.**
65 High Ridge
Rd., #407
Stamford, CT
06905-3806
(203) 359-6925
Contact Toni
Parker

**Blackprint
Heritage Gallery**
162 Edgewood
Ave
New Haven, CT
06511-4522
203-782-2159

Dygnyti Books
828 Dixwell
Avenue
Hamden, CT
06514
(203) 776-9061

Delaware

Haneef's Bookstore
911 N. Orange Street
Wilmington, DE 19801
(302) 656-4193

Florida

African American Heritage Book
515 Northwood Rd; West Palm Beach, FL 33407-5817
561-835-3551

African Book Store
3600 W Broward Blvd
Fort Lauderdale, FL 33312-1014
954-584-0460

Ethnic Elegance
9501 Arlington Expressway
Jacksonville, FL 32225

tel: 904-725-0595
Contact: Reba Johnson

Love Christian Book Store
1968 Bruton Boulevard
Orlando, FL 32805

Nefertiti's Books and Gifts
7640 Lem Turner Boulevard,
Jacksonville, FL 32208
904-766-3630
Contact: Cathy and Naseem Maat

Pyramid Books
544-2 Gateway Blvd.
Boynton Beach, FL. 33535
(561)731-4422 (fax)
(561)731-0202

Tenaj Books &Gift Gallery
608 5. US 1
Fort Pierce, FL

34954
(407) 468-0520
(407) 468-0560 (fax)
Contact: Janet Mosley

Georgia

Celebrate
1015 Patina Pt.
Peachtree City, GA 30269-4013
(404) 486-1338
Contact: Sandra Napper

Heritage Bookstore
2389 Wesley Chapel Rd., Ste. 201
Decatur, GA 30035-2819
(770) 322-7347
Contact: Michele Fenn

Kalors Bookstore
1166 Franklin Road
Suite #6
Marietta, GA 30067

The Shrines of the Black Madonna Bookstore
Atlanta, Ga. 30310
Phone # 404-752-6125
Contact-Ewa or Maia

The Tree of Life Bookstore of Harlem
1701 M.L. King Drive SW
Atlanta, GA 30314-2227
(404) 753-5700
(also fax#)
DrKanya@webtv.net

Two Friends Bookstore
598 Cascade Rd.
Atlanta, GA 30310
(404)758-7711
(404)753-0102
Contact: Renecia Glass

Illinois

Afri-Ware Inc.
948 Lake Str.
Oak Park, IL 60301
(708) 524-8398
(708) 524-8397(fax)
Contact: Jill Bunton
Afriware@aol.com

African American Images Inc
1909 W 95th St
Chicago, IL 60643-1105
312-445-0322

Afrocentric Book Store
234 S. Wabash Ave.
Chicago, IL 60604-2304
(312) 939-1956
Contact: Desiree Sanders

Black Expression Book Source
9500 5 Western Ave
Evergreen Park, IL 60805-2800
708-424-4338

Black Expressions Book Source
17735 Halsted St
Homewood, IL 60430-2095
708-922-1223

Black Titles
35 5 La Salle St
Aurora, IL 60505-3309
630-892-4759

Black Underground Bookstore &Culture Institute
1904 10th St
Waukegan, IL 60085-7161
847-662-6432

The Epicenter Bookshop-UIC
750 S. Halsted St., #M-C048
Chicago, IL 60607-7008
(312) 413-5540
(312) 413-5526 (fax)
Contact Viktor Gliozeris

Indiana

X-Pression
5912 N. College Ave.
Indianapolis, IN 46220-2554
(317) 257-5448
Contact: Donna Stokes-Lucas

Kansas

African American Gifts &Books
2219 E 13th St N
Wichita, KS 67214-1929
316-263-4742

Kentucky

Nimde Books
2200 W. Chestnut Street
Louisville, KY 40211

Louisiana

Black to the Basics Book Store & Gift Shop
311 Main St
Grambling, LA 71245-2724
318-247-8424

Community Book Center
217 N. Broad
New Orleans, LA 70119
(504) 822-2665
Mon-Sat 10am-7pm

Maryland

African American Book Club, Inc.
10606 Cedarwood Ln.
Fort Washington, MD 20744-3948
(912) 328-0682
Contact: Timothy Williams

African American Books And Publishing
2313 W Lafayette Ave
Baltimore, MD 21216-4817
410-945-8429

African-American Books Plus
9485 Timesweep Ln
Columbia, MD 21045-3519
410-730-0779

Ascension Books
5490 Cedar Lane Ste. B3
Columbia, MD 21044
(301) 596-1669
Contact: Ken Williams
ascension-books@usa.net

Black By Popular Demand
5711 Ager Rd
Hyattsville, MD
20782-2602
301-559-8795

HueManity Books
9350 Snowden
River Pkwy.,
Ste. 206
Columbia, MD
21045-5275
(410) 596-6556
Contact: Ellicia
Gamblin

Karibu Books
3500 E. West
Hwy.
Hyattsville, MD
20782-1916
(301) 559-1140
Contact: Brother
Simba

MasterWorks Books
2703 Curry Drive
Adelphi, MD
20783
(301) 422-2168
(301) 422-1289

(fax)
www.mastw.com/
books
Contact: William
Coleman

National Archives
NECA, Library
Rm. 2380
8601 Adelphi Rd.
College Park, MD
20740
(202) 208-7345
Contact: Judy
Edeihoff

Sepia, Sand, & Sable
6796
Reistersttown Rd
Baltimore, MD
21215
(410) 318-8698

Sibayne
4031 Rogers
Avenue
Baltimore, MD
21215
(410) 542-0193

Massachusetts

Afrobooks
927 Main St., #A
Worcester, MA
01610-1429
(508) 799-9799
Contact: Pius Eze

Black Orchid Books
105 Columbia St
Maiden, MA
02148-3017
617-324-0404

Cultural Collections
754 Crescent St.
Brockton, MA
02402-3343
(508) 580-1055
(508) 580-5197
(fax)
Contact: Juliet
Armstrong

Sistahs'
62 Warren St.
Roxbury, MA
02119-3207
(617) 445-9446
Contact: Genita
Johnson

Michigan

Apple Book Center
7900 W. Outer Drive
Detroit, MI 48235
(313) 255-5221
(313) 255-5230
Apple001@aol.com

LaCeter's Book Service
16345 Melrose St.
Southfield, MI 48075
(810) 569-5613
Contact: Sheila Gaddie

Mahogany Books
15768 Biltmore
Detroit, Ml 48227-1558
(313) 273-4479
Contact Teresa Colquitt

Mississippi

The Heritage Center
1103 Martin Luther King Dr.
Vicksburg, MS 39180
(601) 638-8271
Contact: Ezell McDonald

Missouri

Afrocentric Books &Cafe
8081 Olive St
St. Louis, MO 63130
(314) 991-0097

Nebraska

Aframerican Book Store
3226 Lake St
Omaha, NE 68111
(402) 455-9200

New Jersey

African American Book Store
216 1st St
Hackensack, NJ 07601-2400
201-343-0277

African American Boutique
216 1st St
Hackensack, NJ 07601-2400
201-343-0277

African House Institute Of Learning
505 Martin Luther King Jr. Dr
Jersey City, NJ 07304-2307
201-433-0191

BCA Books
P.O. Box 422
Cranbury, NJ
(609) 275-1078
(609) 936-1299 (fax)
Catalogue sales
(800) 995-0064
Contact: Monique or Martin
bcabooks@home.com

Black Pearl Books Plus
P.O. Box 5688
Englewood, NJ

07631-5688
(201) 568-0919
(201) 568-0919
(fax)
Contact: Arlena
Ryland

New York

**A & B
Distributors**
149 Lawrence St.
Brooklyn NY
11217
(718) 596-3389

African Artisans
1211 Grand Ave
Baldwin, NY
11510-1115
516-481-5642

**Black Books
Plus, Inc.**
Author Signings
Only
(212) 749-9632
Contact:
Glenderlyn
Johnson

**Black Mind Book
Boutique**
610 New York

Ave
Brooklyn, NY
11203-1509
718-774-5800

**D &J Book
Distributors**
229-21B Merrick
Blvd.
Laurelton, NY
(718) 949-5400
(718) 949-6161
(fax)

**DARE Books &
Educational
Supplies**
33 Lafayette Ave.
Brooklyn, NY
11217
(718) 625-4651
Contact: Desmond
A. Reid

**Liberation
Bookstore**
421 Malcolm X
Blvd.
New York, NY
10027
(212) 281-4615

**Mood Makers
Books &Art
Gallery**
Village Gate
Square
274 N. Goodman
St.
Rochester, NY
14807
(716) 271-7010
(716) 271-2313
(fax)
Contact: Curtis
Rivers

Nkiru Books
76 St. Marks
Avenue
Brooklyn NY
11217
(718) 783-6306

**Langston Hughes
Community
Library and
Cultural Center**
102-09 Northern
Boulevard
Corona, NY
11368
718 651-1100 and
718 651-7116

**Queens Borough
Public Library**
89-11 Merrick
Blvd.
Jamaica, NY
11432-5248
(718) 990-0721
Contact: John
Oldick

**The Schomburg
Center for
Research into
Black Culture**
(Gift Shop)
515 Malcolm X
Blvd.
New York, NY
10037-1801
(212) 491-2200

**The Studio
Museum of
Harlem**
(Gift Shop)
144 West 125th
St.
New York, NY
10027
(212) 864-4500

**Phenomenal
Sistah Bookstore**
1019 East 212
Street
Suite 100
Bronx, New York
10469
(718) 881 2552
Owner/Contact:
Mamu
URL:
www.psistah.com

North Carolina

**Blacknificent
Books &More**
2011 Poole Rd
Raleigh, NC
27610
919-250-9110

**King Solomon's
Children's
Enterprise**
1308 Thurmond
St.
Winston-Salem,
NC 27105-5731
(910) 723-7706
Contact: Albert
Thombs

Special Occasions
112 N. Martin
Luther King Jr.
Dr.
Winston-Salem,
NC 27101-4407
(919) 724-0334
Contact: E.L.
McCarter

Ohio

**African-
American
Cultural
Exchange**
3640 Mayfield Rd
Cleveland, OH
44118-1403
216-691-3502

**The African
Book Shelf**
1324Q Euclid Ave
Cleveland, OH
44112-4524
216-681-6511

**African &Islamic
Books Plus**
3752 Lee Rd
Cleveland, OH
44128-1410
216-561-5000

Baruti-Ba Books
PO Box 1684
Dayton OH 45401
Contact: Kevin
Tucker

**Brighter Day
Books &Gifts**
5941 Hamilton
Ave.
Cincinnati, OH
45224-3045
(513) 542-6764
Contact: Dolores
Rolland

**A Cultural
Exchange**
12621 Larchmere
Blvd.
Cleveland, OH
44120-1109
(216) 229-8300
(216) 795-5302
(fax)
Contact: Lloyd
McHamm

**Lady Grace
Bookshop**
214 E. Perkins
Ave.
Sandusky, OH
448704376

(419) 621-1991
Contact Grayce
Harmon

Pennsylvania

**Basic Black
Books**
9th and Market
Streets, Mall level
Philadelphia, PA
19107
tel:215/992-4417
Contact: Licia
Bickerstaff

Gene's Books
King of Prussia
Plaza
King of Prussia,
PA 19406-3149
610) 265-6210
610) 265-6260
(fax)
Contact Rashena
Wilson

South Carolina

**Books in the
Black**
7317C Parklane
Rd.
Columbia, SC

29223
(803) 699-9252
Contact: Barbara
Preston

**PowerHouse
Books**
1424 Horreil Hill
Rd.
Hopkins, SC
29061
(803) 785-3032
(803) 785-3065
(fax)
Contact Lovera W.
Robertson

TDIR Books
6920 North Main
Street
Columbia, SC
29203
(803) 754-5911
Toll Free: (888)
246-8211
(803) 754-4922
(fax)

Tennessee

**African
American Gift
Gallery**
114 Carr St.

Knoxville, TN
37919
(423) 584-1320
Contact: Leslie
Valentine

**Alkebu-lan
Images**
2721 Jefferson
Street
Nashville, TN
37208
(615) 321-4111

**Sidewalk
University
International
Booksellers**
2287 Union
Avenue
Memphis, TN
34104
(901) 722-2110
Fax (901) 722-
2112

Texas

**Afro
Awakenings**
2111 Corinth
Street #161
Dallas, TX 75215-
1318

**Babatunde &
Yetunde**
1102 W. Jaspter
Rd.
Killeen, TX 76541
1.877.556-2816
www.uor@killeen
.com

**The Black
Bookworm**
605 E Berry St
Fort Worth, TX
76110-4300
817-923-9661

**The Black
Bookworm**
2300 Ridgeview
St.
Fort Worth, TX
76119-3125
817-535-0366

**Black Images
Book Bazaar**
230 Wynnewood
Village
RO. Box 41059
Dallas, TX 75224
(214) 943-0142
(214) 941-3932
(fax)

Contact: Derrick
Rodgers

**Black Book
Discounters**
4720 La Branch
Houston, Texas
77004
713 520-5188

**Nu World of
Books**
3250 Washington
Blvd.
Beaumont, TX
77705
(409) 842-1412

Virginia

**Cultural
Expression**
P.O. Box 8464
Newport News,
VA 23606-0464
(757) 826-0733
(757) 826-3512
(fax)
Contact: Charlotte
Marie Callins

Washington

Brother's Books
11443 Rainier

Ave. S.
Seattle, WA
98178-3954
(206) 772-0330
(206) 772-7811
(fax)
Contact: Mary
Lou

**Carol's
Essentials Ethnic
Gifts and Books**
1106 23rd Avenue
Seattle,
Washington 98122
(206) 322-9390
(206) 322-
6351(fax)
carolsessentials@e
mail.msn.com

**JUST FROM US
African
American Books**
1851 230TH AVE
NE
Redmond, WA
98053
(425) 836-8297
(425) 836-0781
(fax)
Contact: Marilyn

Washington, D.C.

**Drum and Spear
Books**
556 Varnum Street
NW
Washington, DC
20011
202-722-4758
www.drumandspe
ar.com
Contact: Gigi
Roane, President
Drumandspear.co
m

**Library of
Congress,
Library**
1291 Taylor St.
NW
Washington, DC
20542~001
(202) 707-9234
Contact Caroline
Longmoor

**Martin Luther
King Library**
901 G St NW
Washington, DC
200014599
(202) 727-1117

(202) 727-1129
(fax)
Contact:
Coordinator of
Adult Services

Virtigo Books
1337 Connecticut
Avenue, NW
Washington, DC
20036
(202) 429-9272
(202) 429-9505
Fax

**Sisterspace and
Books**
1354 U Street,
N.W.
Washington, D.C.
20009
(202) 332-3433
(202) 986-7092
(fax)
sistersp@erols.co
m

Yawa Books
2206 18th St. NW
Washington, DC
20009-1813
(202) 483-6805
Contact: Magaji
Bukar

Wisconsin

**Black Swan
Books &Coffee**
765-G Woodlake
Rd
Kohler, WI
53044-1321
414-458-4757

**The Cultural
Connection
Bookstore**

3424 W. Villard
Ave.
Milwaukee, WI
532094710
(414)461-6160
Contact: Frances
Utsey

**The Reader's
Choice**
1950 N. Dr.
Martin Luther
King Jr. Dr.

Milwaukee, WI
53212
(414) 265-2003
(414) 449-9476
(fax)
Contact Carla
Allison

African Book Store

www.africanbookstore.com

Amazon

www.amazon.com

Barnes and Noble

www.bn.com

Black Books Galore

www.blackbooksgalore.com

Black Books Plus

www.blackbooksplus.com

The Book Club House Book Store

www.thebookclubhouse.com

Books-a-Million

www.booksamillion.com

Borders

www.borders.com

Cush City

www.cushcity.com

Just Bookz

www.justbookz.com

Mahogany Books

www.magoganybooks.com

Nia Books

www.niabooks.com

African American Book Store National Directory. www.smallbusinesses.com/bookstore.htm

Burk, Jim. *I Hear America Reading: Why We Read-What We Read.* Heinemann.1999

Covington, Heather. *Literary Divas: The Top 100+Most Admired African American Women in Literature.* Amber Books.2006

Greenwood, Monique. *Go On Girl!: Book Club Guide for Reading Group.* Hyperion. 1999.

Loevy, Dana. The Book Club Companion: A Comprehensive Guide to the Reading Group Experience. Perkey Trade. 2006

Jacobsohn, Rachel W. *The Reading Group Handbook: Everything You Need to Know to Start Your Own Book Club.* Hyperion. 1998

O'Hare, Mary. *Recipe for a Book Club: A Monthly Guide for Hosting Your Own Reading Group: Menus & Recipes, Featured Authors, Suggested Readings, and Topical Questions.* Capitol Books. 2004

Otto, Audra. *The Evolution of American Book Clubs: A Timeline.* www.minnpost.com/bookclubclub/2009/09/15/11501/the_evolutio n_of_american_book_clubs_a_timeline Sept. 15, 2009

Sterling, Dorothy. *We are Your Sistas Black Women in the Nineteenth Century.* W.W. Norton & Co. 1997

Printed Magazines
African American Review
Black Issue Book Review
Booking Matters Magazine
Publisher Weekly